SUPPLEMENTARY STUDIES
for Cornet or Trumpet

To be used with, or to follow any method.

R. M. ENDRESEN

Fingerings for Reference

1

Copyright MCMXXXIV by Rubank Inc., Chicago, Ill.
International Copyright Secured

1

2

Moderato

3

Allegro

4

Valse tempo

5

Allegro

6

Andante

dim.

D. C.

7

Moderato

8

Allegro

9

Andante

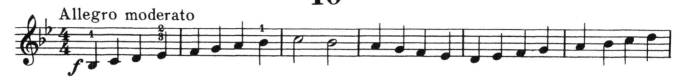

10

Allegro moderato

11

S. S. for Cor. or Trpt.

12

Scherzando

Fine

D. C.

13

Allegro

14

In strict rhythm

15

Moderato

16

Andante sostenuto

17

Allegretto

18

Allegro moderato

19

20

March time

21

Allegretto

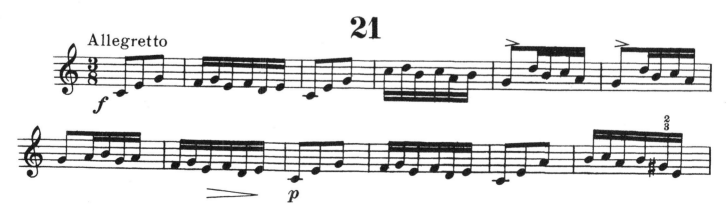

22

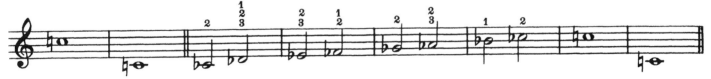

23

24

25

March tempo

28

29

30

31

32

33

34